YORKSHIRE DALES

Photographed by Andrew Lambert

SALMON

Introduction

The Yorkshire Dales is one of the finest upland areas of Britain combining an unspoilt landscape with a rich local history. Airedale, Wharfedale, Nidderdale, Wensleydale and Swaledale are the best known of the dales, but into each of these run smaller dales each with their own unique charm and delights. The well-known image of the dales of secluded valleys bisected by drystone walls and dotted with isolated barns is still at the heart of the area's appeal, but within the landscape majestic ruined castles and abbeys and peaceful villages all add to its interest. To the west the famous peaks of Pen-y-ghent, Ingleborough and Whernside provide a more desolate aspect as the gentler dales scenery gives way to wild moorland. Despite their popularity it is easy to find peace and solitude within the dales, whether beside a rushing waterfall, amongst the ruins of an abbey church or on a quiet footpath and it is this which continues to give this unique area its appeal.

An autumnal day at Bolton Abbey

Springtime beside the pack-horse bridge, Linton

The village pond at Addingham, Lower Wharfedale

Upper Wharfedale near Buckden

Kilnsey Crag stands 170 feet high

Two views of Burnsall from the Struff Road, in autumn and winter

The Strid, Bolton Woods

Park Falls in Desolation Valley, Wharfedale

Barden Tower near Bolton Abbey was originally a medieval hunting lodge

Summertime in Wharfedale near Kettlewell

Simon's Seat and Skyreholme, Wharfedale

A blanket of snow covers Wharfedale near Barden Bridge

The village square at Grassington

Kettlewell village

A winter's day at Kettlewell

Hubberholme lies at the entrance to Littondale

Arncliffe village nestles in Littondale

22

Malham Cove is a 250 feet high wall of rock rising above the River Aire

The dramatic gorge at Gordale Scar, near Malham

The limestone pavement above Malham Cove

An ancient pack-horse bridge spans the Malham Beck

High Street, Skipton

Pen-y-ghent and Settle

Buttercups carpet the churchyard at Horton-in-Ribblesdale

Glacial drumlins dominate the landscape between Ribblehead and Ingleborough

Massive Pen-y-ghent dominates the Ribble Valley

The River Ribble at Stainforth

Springtime at St. Mary's Church, Ingleton

Ingleborough from the limestone pavement

The Waterfalls Walk at Thornton Force, Ingleton

A tree-lined beck flows through Claph

There is a fine view of Dentdale from the summit of Whernside

St. Andrew's Church and village, Dent

The Sun Inn and Sedgwick Stone stand in the village of Dent

Caultey Spout waterfall near Sedbergh

Sedbergh is the western gateway to the Dales

The Middle and Upper Falls at Aysgarth, Wensleydale

"*All Creatures Great and Small*" was filmed in Askrigg village

There are fine views of Wensleydale from the ramparts of Bolton Castle

West Burton Cauldron

The village of West Burton lies in Bishopdale

The ruins of Jervaulx Abbey

The keep of Middleham Castle dates from the 12th century

Hardraw Force plunges 96 feet

The Gayle Beck, Hawes

The village of Gunnerside nestles among the meadows of Upper Swaledale

Thwaite village, Swaledale

Cottages at Muker

Shops and inns surround the village green at Reeth

Richmond Castle from the River Swale

Kisdon Force near Keld

The River Swale cascades over ledges at Wain Wath Force

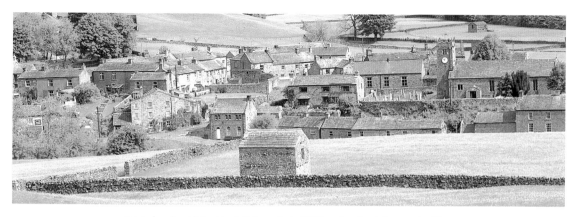

Printed and published by J. Salmon Ltd., 100 London Road, Sevenoaks, Kent.
Telephone: 01732 452381   Email: enquiries@jsalmon.co.uk   Website: www.jsalmon.co.uk

ISBN 1 84640 031 7

First edition 2006

Front cover: Swaledale, back cover: Clapham, page one: Pateley Bridge, page two: Aysgarth Falls
page sixty-two: Swaledale, page sixty-three: Muker, page sixty-four: Janet's Foss